The First Battle of Kiev: The History of Disastrous Defeat of W(

By Charles River I

A picture of German artillery around Kiev after the battle (this picture and the book cover come from the Bundesarchiv)

About Charles River Editors

Charles River Editors is a boutique digital publishing company, specializing in bringing history back to life with educational and engaging books on a wide range of topics. Keep up to date with our new and free offerings with this 5 second sign up on our weekly mailing list, and visit Our Kindle Author Page to see other recently published Kindle titles.

We make these books for you and always want to know our readers' opinions, so we encourage you to leave reviews and look forward to publishing new and exciting titles each week.

Introduction

A depiction of Kiev after the battle

The First Battle of Kiev

"We have only to kick in the door and the whole rotten structure will come crashing down." – Adolf Hitler

In the warm predawn darkness of June 22, 1941, 3 million men waited along a front hundreds of miles long, stretching from the Baltic coast of Poland to the Balkans. Ahead of them in the darkness lay the Soviet Union, its border guarded by millions of Red Army troops echeloned deep throughout the huge spaces of Russia. This massive gathering of Wehrmacht soldiers from Adolf Hitler's Third Reich and his allied states – notably Hungary and Romania – stood poised to carry out Operation Barbarossa, Hitler's surprise attack against the country of his putative ally, Soviet dictator Josef Stalin.

At precisely 1:00 a.m. that morning, the radios of command and headquarter units all along the line crackled to life. Officers and generals heard a single code word: "Dortmund" for Army Group North, and "Wotan," the name of the one-eyed pre-Christian god of knowledge, war, and runes, for Army Group South. In answer to shouted orders and tactical-level radio transmissions, men threw aside camouflage nets, truck, halftrack, and panzer engines started with a throbbing rumble, and artillerists prepared their weaponry for the terrific barrage generally preceding a

Wehrmacht assault. Soldiers swarmed onto trains, and the propellers of thousands of German aircraft, including the still-formidable Stuka dive-bombers, roared amid the nighttime stillness on dozens of airfields throughout Eastern Europe.

Though Germany was technically Russia's ally, Stalin had no delusions that they were friends. Instead, he used this time to build up his forces for what he saw as an inevitable invasion. First, on the heels of the German invasion of Poland in September 1939, Stalin had his troops invade and reclaim the land Russia had lost in World War I. Next he turned his attention to Finland, which was only 100 miles from the newly named Leningrad. He initially tried to negotiate with the Finnish government for some sort of treaty of mutual support. When this failed he simply invaded. While the giant Russian army ultimately won, the fact that little Finland held them off for three months demonstrated how poorly organized the bigger force was.

Initially, Stalin believed he had several years to build up his army before Germany would invade, figuring it would at least take the Germans that long to conquer France and Britain. However, when France fell quickly in 1940, it seemed he might have miscalculated, so he again sent Molotov to Berlin to stall for time. Meanwhile, Hitler trained his sights on Britain, turning his attention to destroying the Royal Air Force as a prerequisite for the invasion of Britain.

The British were able to prevent a German invasion thanks to the Battle of Britain in late 1940, and Stalin knew that if he could delay an invasion through the summer of 1941, he would be safe for another year. Unfortunately for Stalin, Molotov's mission to Berlin failed and Hitler began to plan to invade Russia by May of 1941. Since military secrets are typically the hardest to keep, Stalin soon began to hear rumors of the invasion, but even when Winston Churchill contacted him in April of 1941 warning him that German troops seemed to be massing on Russia's border, Stalin remained dubious. Stalin felt even more secure in his position when the Germans failed to invade the following May.

What Stalin did not realize was that Hitler had simply over stretched himself in Yugoslavia and only planned to delay the invasion by a few weeks. Hitler aimed to destroy Stalin's Communist regime, but he also hoped to gain access to resources in Russia, particularly oil. Throughout the first half of 1941, Germany dug in to safeguard against an Allied invasion of Western Europe as it began to mobilize millions of troops to invade the Soviet Union. Stalin even refused to believe the report of a German defector who claimed that the troops were massing on the Soviet border at that very moment.

The Soviets were so caught by surprise at the start of the attack that the Germans were able to push several hundred miles into Russia across a front that stretched dozens of miles long, reaching the major cities of Leningrad and Sevastopol in just three months. The first major Russian city in their path was Minsk, which fell in only six days. In order to make clear his determination to win at all costs, Stalin had the three men in charge of the troops defending

Minsk executed for their failure to hold their position. This move, along with unspeakable atrocities by the German soldiers against the people of Minsk, solidified the Soviet will. In the future, Russian soldiers would fight to the death rather than surrender, and in July, Stalin exhorted the nation, "It is time to finish retreating. Not one step back! Such should now be our main slogan. ... Henceforth the solid law of discipline for each commander, Red Army soldier, and commissar should be the requirement — not a single step back without order from higher command."

Though the attack caught Stalin utterly by surprise, the tension between the two violent, predatory states made such a clash almost inevitable. The USSR had no plans to invade Germany in 1941, but it had remained an aggressive military state infused with the savage zeal to abolish all borders into one international "workers' paradise" through force of arms, as Vladimir Lenin (and many other Soviet leaders and writers) made clear: "Bourgeois nationalism and proletarian internationalism – they are two irreconcilably hostile slogans [...] We say yes to any struggle against national oppression. For any struggle for any kind of national development, for 'national culture' in general, we say unconditionally no." (Ellis, 2015, 90).

Hitler, for his part, wanted Lebensraum for the Germans – at the expense, of course, of the Slavs – and viewed the communist state as an existential threat to Europe itself. Driven by a mix of raw acquisitive ambition, ideology, and actual understanding of the Soviet Union's own minatory intent, the Fuhrer launched a full-scale invasion. Likely with intentional malice, the declaration of war delivered by Gustav von Schulenburg several hours after the invasion's start mirrored almost exactly the Soviet pretext of "defending their borders" used during the USSR's invasions of Poland, Latvia, Lithuania, and Finland: "In view of the intolerable further threats which have been created for the eastern German borders as a consequence of the massed concentration and preparation of all the armed forces of the Red Army, the German government considers itself compelled immediately to take military countermeasures." (Ellis, 2015, 161-162). Thus, Hitler had cast aside his uneasy, friction laden alliance with the Soviet Union, striking it while the Red Army remained debilitated by Stalin's purges of the officer corps and his destruction of mobile tank doctrine as "counterrevolutionary."

In beginning the start of the fighting on the Eastern Front, the deadliest part of history's deadliest war, Operation Barbarossa would turn out to be arguably the most fateful choice of World War II. And while just about everyone knows the end result today, things looked tenuous for the Soviets within just weeks of the start of the invasion. The German High Command split the invading forces into three major groupings – Army Group North, Army Group Center, and Army Group South. Army Group Center initially represented the main effort – the focal point, or Schwerpunkt, of the entire campaign.

Backed by extremely shrewd and professionally executed logistics arrangements based on rapidly-advanced railways, Army Group Center plunged forward through Minsk, then Smolensk, like an arrow aimed at Moscow, a crucial Soviet rail hub and manufacturing center. The Wehrmacht's leadership initially tasked Army Groups North and South with guarding the flanks of Army Group Center. They, too, smashed forward through Soviet defenses, but only as secondary operations supporting the main thrust.

However, as the Germans began taking Smolensk, Hitler suddenly diverted significant forces to the northern and southern flanks. Heinz Guderian's Panzer Group 2 found itself sent to assist in the Ukraine rather than smashing directly through to Moscow. The diversion of this force increased the scope of the Kiev encirclement and the eventual haul of prisoners, but Guderian himself opposed it: "Hoth and myself – in contradiction to this – were anxious to continue the advance eastwards with our panzer forces according to the original, expressed intentions of the supreme command, and to capture the objective initially assigned to us." (Guderian, 1996, 166-167).

Nevertheless, once given his orders, Guderian carried them out with the typical high degree of professionalism characterizing the Wehrmacht. Despite the logistical difficulties generated by the new emphasis on a rapid advance in the south, and the stubborn, courageous, but disastrously uncoordinated resistance of the Red Army, the Germans succeeded in winning the gigantic struggle for Kiev and the Ukraine.

While the First Battle of Kiev represented an operational triumph for the Germans, resulting in an astounding number of Red Army prisoners and the complete collapse of the Ukraine's defenses, the victory came at a high price. Hitler's diversion of Heinz Guderian's Panzer Group II south from the Army Group Center Schwerpunkt increased the power and effectiveness of the Kiev encirclement, but cast away the near certainty of taking Moscow itself in August. Meanwhile, for their part, the Soviets tried hard to forget the disastrous battle ever occurred, going so far as to omit its mention in subsequent histories of the war.

The First Battle of Kiev: The History of the Soviet Red Army's Most Disastrous Defeat of World War II analyzes the strategic implications of the climactic battle. Along with pictures of important people and places, you will learn about the battle like never before.

The First Battle of Kiev: The History of the Soviet Red Army's Most Disastrous Defeat of World War II

About Charles River Editors

Introduction

   Chapter 1: The Start of Operation Barbarossa

   Chapter 2: The Drive East

   Chapter 3: The Fighting Outside of Kiev

   Chapter 4: Initial Assaults on Kiev

   Chapter 5: The Arrival of Guderian

   Chapter 6: The Encirclement and Fall of Kiev

   Chapter 7: The Aftermath of the Battle

   Online Resources

   Bibliography

Free Books by Charles River Editors

Discounted Books by Charles River Editors

Chapter 1: The Start of Operation Barbarossa

Hitler likely intended to attack the Soviet Union since the beginning of his expansionism in the late 1930s. However, actual planning for Operation Barbarossa, the invasion of the USSR, began only in the summer of 1940. After splitting Poland with the eastern dictatorship in 1939, Hitler's Third Reich conquered France and the Low Countries in 1940, and it was not yet known how the Battle of Britain would play out. Nonetheless, Hitler was already thinking about the conquest of the Soviet Union.

The important artillery general Erich Marcks, later killed by an Allied fighter-bomber attack in Normandy, drew up the initial plan in August 1940. This plan envisioned two army groups, Army Groups North and South, advancing into the USSR on either side of the immense Pripet Marshes, the largest obstacle in western Russia. Soon, however, the Germans scrapped this plan in favor of a more flexible arrangement with three army groups. Army Group North, under Field Marshal Ritter von Leeb, would push for Leningrad, while Army Group Center would drive for Moscow under the leadership of Field Marshal Fedor von Bock. This formation represented the largest and best-supplied portion of the Barbarossa invasion, given its centrally important task, and while both of these army groups operated north of the Pripet Marshes, to the south of the Pripet morass, the prickly Field Marshal Gerd von Rundstedt headed Army Group South, charged with advancing through the Ukraine, taking Kiev and the Dnieper River, and preventing Soviet counterattacks from reaching the indispensable Romanian oil fields.

Marcks

Leeb

Bock

The main thrust would lie along the axis to Moscow, according to original plans. While often compared to Napoleon Bonaparte's doomed incursion into Russia in 1812, the comparison is facile and fails to correspond to historical reality. Moscow in 1812 represented a large tract of buildings with symbolic and shelter value, but nothing more, whereas in the technological world of 1941, the Russian capital stood as the pulsing nerve center of the Soviet Union's European region – a region containing most of the USSR's population, factories, and armies. Wehrmacht panzer general Heinz Guderian spoke accurately of "the geographical significance of Moscow, which was quite different from that of, say, Paris. Moscow was the great Russian road, rail, and communications centre: it was the political solar plexus: it was an important industrial area: and its capture would not only have an enormous psychological effect on the Russian people but on the whole rest of the world as well." (Guderian, 1996, 199).

Stalin's Red Army, for all its deficiencies, represented a modern fighting force for its day, infinitely different from the Czar's armies in 1812. The Soviet armies required massive logistical support along railways in the same manner as the Germans – which is a major reason why the Wehrmacht's encircling tactics had such a devastating effect on the Red Army in 1941. Cut off from steady supply of gasoline, diesel, ammunition, reinforcements, and food in vast quantities, the Red Army units quickly became a starving rabble on foot, with their trucks, aircraft, and tanks immobilized by lack of fuel. In fact, once they drove the Germans back west late in the war, the Soviets laid Russian-gauge railways into eastern and central Europe. Without the arteries of the railways infusing them with the varied lifeblood of war materiel, the Red Army divisions in 1944 and 1945 would have quickly halted, perhaps permanently.

Organized by a centralized totalitarian state, the Soviet rail network in the west used Moscow as the hub for practically every major rail line. The capital's colossal mustering yards maintained the rolling stock that moved all supplies to the front. Thus, had the Germans seized Moscow, this one act would cut off the northern and southern Red Army units from all ammunition, fuel, food, and reinforcements. In a matter of days, most tanks and other vehicles would cease to work, eliminating Soviet mobility on even the tactical scale. No reinforcements could reach any point beyond Moscow, and building new rail lines would take months if it proved possible at all.

As a result, control of Moscow would defeat all Soviet forces in European Russia rapidly and totally, while placing strategic and operational initiative in the Germans' hands. Moscow would provide a superb base for the winter, and the Soviet state – already loathed by most of its subjects, who understandably resented its murderous character, seizure of their property, and aggressive atheism – might well collapse. Moscow, then, represented a viable target, probably offering the key to defeating the Soviet Union in the first summer's campaign, or at least reducing it to an impotent rump state in Siberia that would likely be forced to sue for peace.

Still, the sheer size and difficult terrain of Russia presented the Wehrmacht with a vast logistical challenge, which even the Fuhrer understood. According to the war journal of Generaloberst Franz Halder of the general staff, Hitler decided to send all available anti-aircraft artillery (AAA) to support Barbarossa rather than protecting Germany proper (which would be guarded by fighter planes), indicating the Fuhrer's intention to fully commit necessary resources to the plan: "AA defense will be slightly weakened (30%) in favor of Barbarossa. [...] AAA: Fuehrer wants no serviceable piece to remain inactive. Personnel for 30 Batteries. AA Corps, of 6 [Battalions], for 6th Army ([Armored] Group 1) and [Armored] Group 2." (Halder, , 9).

This decision had a notably positive effect on operations both by providing extra flak cover for the panzer spearheads of Army Groups Center and South, and by ensuring a large number of 8.8 FlaK 36 or 37 anti-aircraft cannons on the ground in Russia. The 88mm flak gun, or "Eighty-Eight," represented the only German gun deployed in 1941 which reliably penetrated the armor of KV-1 and KV-2 tanks.

Halder further notes that the Ostheer (Eastern Army) ensured "15,000 Polish peasant carts with drivers will be made ready for Barbarossa by beginning of May," (Halder, , 34) thus ensuring that slow but effective transport, adapted to low quality Eastern European roads, would be available to the invasion force.

The Wehrmacht actually anticipated the logistical challenges of the USSR's large spaces with considerable clarity, including the lack of European-gauge railroads in the east. Though the army planned for an operation ending with the capture of Moscow in late summer or early autumn – thus neglecting winter gear – the quartermaster corps stockpiled large amounts of supplies for the summer campaign, assembled materials and pioneers to drive railroads rapidly into Soviet territory, and built up a pool of tens of thousands of tons (in cargo capacity) of trucks in 60-ton convoys.

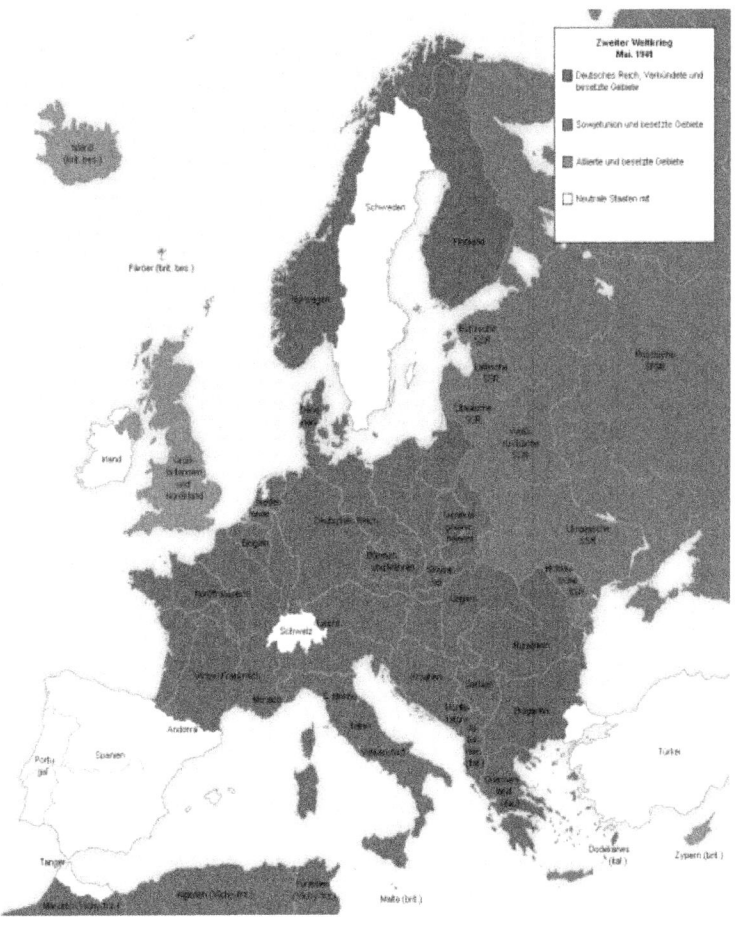

The borders of Europe ahead of Operation Barbarossa

Army Group Center provided the *Schwerpunkt*, or focal point, of the Barbarossa operation. Though the other two army groups each aimed for important objectives, Army Group Center aimed for the biggest prize of 1941: Moscow itself, via Minsk and Smolensk. This could bring about possible victory for the Germans that very summer.

For this reason, Army Group Center received the most men, the strongest logistical support, and two panzer groups, Panzer Groups II and III. Heinz Guderian, a thorny and annoying man but one of the Wehrmacht's finest armor generals, led Panzer Group II. Colonel-General Hermann "Papa" Hoth, commanding Panzer Group III, represented another highly competent commander, though one less historically famous. Field Marshal Fedor von Bock commanded Army Group Center overall.

Guderian

The Germans moved men to the front from the start of 1941 on, though only a trickle of divisions arrived in the winter. The pace of deployment accelerated in March and exploded in April. Originally, Hitler planned to launch Operation Barbarossa in mid-May 1941. However, due to an extremely wet spring which softened vast areas of terrain and swelled several rivers in the direct path of Army Group Center's and South's advance, the Fuhrer postponed the invasion until June 22nd. The last deployment started on May 23rd, one month before the launch of the attack.

Though the Germans did their best to conceal the preparations for Barbarossa through a variety of methods, mustering a heavily (though not fully) mechanized army of 3 million men could not be concealed. News arrived at the Soviet headquarters in Moscow from a wide range of sources, yet Stalin authorized no additional preparations for a potential Third Reich attack on the Soviet Union.

The murderous, primitive paranoia of the Soviet leader goes a long way in explaining this situation. Starting in 1939 and continuing into 1940, the Soviet dictator began systematically destroying his own foreign intelligence apparatus. Suspecting treachery from men who actually put their entire effort into helping Russia with intelligence gathering, Stalin repeatedly changed the intelligence chiefs at home, each previous occupant of the office dying in NKVD torture chambers or cells. Worse, Stalin had numerous agents in Europe and elsewhere in the world recalled to the USSR. When they arrived, the NKVD arrested them, tortured bizarre confessions out of them, and shot them in their underground cells, often after circus-like, sadistic show trials. The NKVD infiltrated death squads into Western Europe to assassinate those spies who defected rather than return to certain torture and execution.

The reason for this strange procedure lay in Stalin's conviction that anyone who visited the West would be suborned by capitalism and must therefore be a traitor and double agent. This had the effect of collapsing the Soviets' spy networks and casting their reports (actually, in most cases, highly accurate) into doubt in Stalin's mind.

Despite the purges, Soviet intelligence officers still reported the coming invasion weeks ahead of time. The leading Soviet agent in Japan, Richard Sorge, posed as an undercover German journalist and received brief but useful advance warning of Barbarossa. A newly arrived German officer, Lieutenant Colonel Erwin Scholl, confided a highly specific outline of the plan to Sorge over an elegant dinner at the Imperial Hotel, talking under cover of orchestral music played for the guests' entertainment. Sorge sent off a radio message to Moscow on June 1st: "Expected start of German-Soviet war on June 15th is based exclusively on information which Lieutenant-Colonel Scholl brought with him from Berlin, which he left on May 6 heading for Bangkok. He is taking up post of attache in Bangkok. Ott stated he could not receive information on this subject directly from Berlin, and only has Scholl's information." (Whymant, 1996, 167).

Sorge

The Soviet government had ordered Sorge to return to the USSR, but by guessing correctly that he would be arrested, tortured for a few days, and then killed, the agent offered a variety of excuses to postpone his return, and he still remained deeply loyal to Russia, if not the Soviet regime, thus supplying all the high quality information he could gather. Stalin, however, dismissed the warning. Having described Sorge as "a shit who has set himself up with some small factories and brothels in Japan" (Whymant, 1996, 184), the dictator and his henchmen sent back a terse reply accusing Sorge of lying.

In addition to Soviet agents, Red Army commanders near the border repeatedly sounded the alarm to Stalin, attempting to prompt the Soviet leader to authorize the movement of reinforcements up to the border. Lieutenant Fyodor Arkhipenko described the Stavka (Soviet GHQ) response to signs of German war preparations: "In the spring of 1941, German reconnaissance planes constantly violated our border and conducted […] flights over the Soviet territory and our airfield, but there were instructions not to shoot them down and not even to scare them, but only escort them to the border. Everything was done as to postpone the war, prevent the development of attempted German provocation." (Kamenir, 2008, 69).

Additionally, since at least April 1941, the British also provided the Soviets with detailed information from their own excellent intelligent network about the impending Operation Barbarossa. The British officers providing this data to Soviets in England found themselves met with suspicious, hostile, and contemptuous questioning. Due to the earlier threat of the British to send troops to aid the Finns against the Soviet invasion of 1939-1940, and the fact that the English represented two-dimensional capitalists and thus foes in Stalin's eyes, the Soviets assumed the British and Germans worked in cahoots, actually labeling the invaluable data offered "provocation."

The use of the word "provocation" perhaps grants insight about Stalin's reasons for stubbornly refusing to believe the burgeoning flood of intelligence pointing to an imminent massive German invasion of the USSR – a mix of paranoia, arrogance, and self-delusion. Marshal Georgi Zhukov noted that Stalin's mass liquidation of the Soviet officer corps had gutted the Red Army's fighting prowess, and that "J.V. Stalin clearly knew as well that after 1939, military units were led by commanders far from being well-versed in operational-tactical and strategic education. […] It was also impossible to discount the moral traumas which were inflicted upon the Red Army and Navy by the massive purges." (Kamenir, 2008, 58).

Zhukov

Leading commissar Nikita Khrushchev, the man who eventually replaced Stalin as Soviet premier, provided a final piece of the puzzle of Stalin's actions by recording in the first volume of his memoirs the abject, helpless terror that the actual invasion plunged Stalin into. His extraordinary description is either full-blown calumny, or the portrait of a man driven into paralytic terror and despair by the arrival of an event he had dreaded but managed to delude himself would never happen: "Stalin was completely crushed. His morale was shattered, and he made the following declaration: 'The war has begun. It will develop catastrophically. Lenin left us the proletarian Soviet state, but we have sh— all over it' […] He walked out […] and went to his dacha nearest the city. […] When we came to his dacha [...] I could see from his face that Stalin was very frightened. I suppose that Stalin was thinking we had come there to arrest him." (Khrushchev, 2005, 304).

Khrushchev

While knowing precisely what Stalin thought is impossible, these varied facts may reveal the dictator's motivation. Stalin knew that he had destroyed his own army's fighting power and felt profound fear that a war would start, he would be blamed for the subsequent disaster, and this would cause his downfall and execution. Accordingly, he adopted a pose of doing absolutely nothing that might trigger the Germans to attack, hoping to gain time to build more tanks and train new officers. In addition, he went about killing his own agents who warned of Barbarossa, and dismissing the British intelligence as "provocation," in a panicky effort to deny the possibility of his worst fears being realized even to himself.

Regardless of the exact reasons – either terrified delusion, arrogant overestimation of the Red Army's fighting capabilities, or some other cause – Stalin refused to allow the units at the border to prepare for attack. He also disallowed reinforcements even on a local level. Some commanders secretly moved a few of their rear echelon units up to the border in an effort to strengthen its defenses. They did so in secret, however, because their actions could be labeled "panic-mongering" – a type of sabotage – which could lead to anything from a simple Stavka countermanding of the order, to dismissal from their command, to outright execution.

Chapter 2: The Drive East

Thanks to the tactical and strategic surprise, the Nazis quickly pushed hundreds of miles east into Soviet territory in the span of just a few weeks. After the fall of Smolensk on July 16th, Army Group Center had advanced 440 miles from its starting position in a period of just 25 days. This represented 66% of the way to Moscow; only 220 miles still separated the Germans from their objective. Additionally, the Army Group mustered some 50 mostly intact divisions, while the Soviets only had 26 divisions still available for the defense of Moscow. During the following days, up to August 5th, the Germans battled hard to eliminate the Red Army forces caught in the Smolensk pocket. By the end of the fight, the Soviets had lost another 3,200 tanks, 3,000 artillery pieces, 1,000 aircraft, and 302,000 prisoners to the Germans.

With Smolensk taken, the Germans drove rapidly forward and took Yelnia, creating a salient into Soviet lines. It was at this moment that Hitler's strange tendency to shy away from the culminating stroke of a military victory emerged. In France in 1940, Hitler twice halted decisive offensives and diverted the troops to secondary objectives, as if fearful of the risk of a climactic battle – or perhaps fearing success itself. He halted Guderian's drive to the coast in France, and then stopped the attack on Dunkirk until too late, missing the opportunity to deal the English a crippling blow both in human losses and morale.

With practically all of his men and officers straining forward, eager to be unleashed against Moscow, the Fuhrer suddenly decided to send Guderian south to help take Kiev and Hoth north to seize Leningrad, thus utterly dissipating the juggernaut-like onrush of Army Group Center. Hitler's generals protested strenuously, but the Fuhrer merely replied contemptuously that his commanders did not understand economics or politics. Of course, Hitler himself completely overlooked the economic and political consequences of *losing*, as the Germans might well do if they failed to capture the nerve center of Moscow and deal a fatal blow to the Soviet Union west of the Caucasus.

After much protest, Hitler allowed Hoth's men to remain with Army Group Center. Guderian's Panzer Group II, however, would find itself sent south to waste precious weeks helping Army Group South fight for Kiev. The Soviets lacked any significant tank strength between Smolensk and Moscow during the rest of 1941 – and in fact, the German vehicles now outnumbered the utterly decimated Soviet machines by a factor of 2:1 in this region.

The First Battle of Kiev ultimately emerged from both the natural progress of Army Group South eastward and of Hitler's decision on August 3rd to turn Heinz Guderian's Panzer Group II south. These orders halted the rapid drive to Moscow which the German general staff planned for August and early September – the time when this decisive maneuver would probably succeed, given the temporary lack of Soviet strategic reserves and the good summer weather. The start of the battle of Kiev therefore also marked the exact moment when Hitler aborted Barbarossa's best chance for success, as Fedor von Bock pointed out: "Only in one place on the eastern front – in front of Army Group Center – is the enemy really smashed. […] Now is the time to attack with all of the mobile troops toward Moscow." (Stolfi, 1992, 76).

Army Group South had mustered 46.5 divisions at the start of the campaign, mostly German units but also Romanians, totaling over 700,000 men. Two crack SS divisions strengthened the already tough, formidable Wehrmacht soldiery: Leibstandarte Adolf Hitler (LAH), then not strictly a division but expanded to de facto divisional strength, and Wiking, including Danes, Norwegians, Flemings, and Dutch alongside Germans. Matched against these commanders and soldiers, the Soviet Southwestern Front had initially consisted of 907,000 men and more than 4,000 tanks, commanded by Colonel-General Mikhail Kirponos. A Ukrainian by national origin, Kirponos displayed more military competence than most of his contemporary Soviet peers. The barbaric cavalryman Semyon Mikhailovich Budyonny commanded the whole region, while Nikita Khrushchev served as the Kiev area's chief political commissar, enjoying a good working relationship with Kirponos but finding himself at odds with Budyonny and even Josef Stalin.

Army Group South drove east towards Kiev at considerable speed, using the shock and maneuver tactics of the early-war Wehrmacht to the full against the unprepared Soviet defenders. Cities such as Vinnytsia and Lviv, the latter the center of the Galicia region, fell rapidly into German hands during this onrush.

As the Ostheer (Eastern Army) units pushed into the Ukraine, they encountered different conditions than those prevailing in Belarus. The primitive road networks and other problems would soon strain the Wehrmacht's logistics severely, but the Germans managed to continue their advance nevertheless, despite the lack of the massive rail-building effort supporting Army Group Center. General Gotthard Heinrici described the people and conditions the Germans encountered while advancing towards Kiev: "There are only a very few major roads, and all by-road bridges are destroyed. The weather is still very warm, the roads are finally solid. Instead of being sandy like in Belarus, they are clay here in the Ukraine. The people are better dressed. For weeks have seen women running around with bare legs, here they wear high boots. […] Everyone chews sunflower seeds, we too. We have seen large quantities of cattle." (Hurter, 2014, 81).

The weather varied between dusty summer heat and violent storms, the latter temporarily slowing advance by turning the roads into quagmires. The supply situation remained acceptable at this time, however. Army Group South only experienced localized ammunition shortages twice during the Battle of Kiev, in both cases due to the tactical situation (Soviet units blocking deliveries) rather than an overall logistical breakdown.

The Germans drove a single railway forward to support Army Group South, less than intended, and less than the multiple rail lines feeding supplies to Army Group Center at the same time. However, the southern advance, at this time, still represented a secondary, supporting theater, meant chiefly to assist Army Group Center's drive. Real supply difficulties began only when

Army Group South operated well east of the Dnieper River, which blocked easy rail and road resupply.

Despite the difficulty and lack of focus on this region, Army Group South still moved at a surprisingly fast speed. The Western Bug River formed much of Army Group South's initial border with the Soviets, blocking Panzer Group I under Ewald von Kleist until the combat engineers constructed two large pontoon bridges across the flow. Kleist, a highly skilled, personally brave, and relatively benevolent officer, was later charged by the Soviets with the "war crime" of suborning Soviet citizens by acting towards them with "friendship and generosity."

On the other side, Lieutenant General Mikhail Kirponos, commanding the Southwestern Front – one of the two Red Army fronts in the Ukraine – found himself defending with a sizable portion of the USSR's 1941 tank force, due to Stalin's conviction the *Schwerpunkt* would occur in the south, but such an abysmally poor communications network that he could not establish even a modicum of control until June 24th, two days after Barbarossa started.

Kirponos

Though the Soviets launched armored counterattacks against Army Group South as early as June 23rd, these often developed in an extremely amateurish fashion, squandering the potential of the heavily-armored and well-armed T-34, KV-1, and KV-2 tanks. In one instance, Oberleutnant

Edel Zachariae-Lingenthal with five Panzer III tanks managed to drive off a column of T-34s with ineffective, non-penetrating hits which nevertheless seemingly unnerved the inexperienced crews: "Even though at this short distance every shot was a hit, the Russians drove on without much visible effect... Despite repeated hits, our fire had no effect. It appears as if shells are simply bouncing off. The enemy tanks disengaged without fighting and retreated." (Forczyk, 2013, 57).

Major General Sergei Ogurtsov followed up this abortive push with the first major Soviet tank attack in the Ukraine, throwing 100 tanks and two battalions of motorized infantry against Gustav-Adolf Riebel's Panzer Regiment 15 near Radekhov. The German panzers, supported by field artillery and antitank guns, pulverized Ogurtsov's initial wave of light T-26 tanks and armored cars.

When the second wave, consisting of early-model T-34 tanks, moved in, the Germans found themselves in a sticky situation. The Panzer III and IV tanks – the latter still lacking the 7.5cm KwK 40 L/43 gun capable of knocking out T-34s, which only appeared in the field in the Ausf. F version of 1942 – could not damage these Soviet armored fighting vehicles. While the artillery disabled some by hitting their tracks – an unsatisfactory solution – the Germans only routed Ogurtsov's attack when the Panzer IV crews fired their grenade launchers at close range, setting the fuel drums carried on the T-34s' rear decks ablaze.

The Soviets continued to launch small, piecemeal armor attacks throughout late June and into early July, depleting their tank reserves without seriously hampering the Germans. Wehrmacht units cast out numerous motorized recon detachments, found the weak points between Soviet divisions, then penetrated these to envelop the luckless Red Army soldiers. Within a few days, Army Group South crushed Stalin's border defenses.

The Germans worked hard to break through and achieve operational freedom of movement, essential to the successful application of mobile warfare or "Blitzkrieg." On top of that, a particular bugbear of the Southwest Front existed in the person of Corps Commissar N.N. Vashugin. This power-drunk zealot, with a military tribunal and a platoon of NKVD killers in tow, haunted the headquarters of various units, beginning with Kirponos' own and extending down to local commanders attempting to stop the Germans. Vashugin proved an able, if unwitting, helper to the Wehrmacht, terrorizing and dominating the leaders facing Army Group South, demoralizing them with constant accusations and threats of execution, and ordering suicidally incompetent attacks over the objections of more knowledgeable men.

On June 27th, the advancing Germans of Ewald von Kleist's Panzer Group I, along with infantry of Hyazinth von Strachwitz, became embroiled in heavy fighting near Dubno and Brody, in a battle variously known as the Battle of Dubno, the Battle of Brody, or the Battle of Rovno. The Soviets deployed some 3,500 tanks of the 10th Tank Division and the 4th, 8th, 15th, 19th, and 22nd Mechanized Corps in an attempted encircling attack. The battle continued through

June 30th, with 750 German panzers matched against 3,500 Soviet tanks, including a total of 717 T-34 and KV tanks, nearly half of the existing stock of these heavier tanks in the Red Army arsenal of mid-1941. Franz Halder's war journal notes, "Army Group South reports still heavy fighting. On the right shoulder of Armored Group 1, behind the sector of Eleventh Armored Div., a deep penetration by Russian Eighth Armored Corps in our lines, apparently has caused a lot of confusion in the area between Brody and Dubno and temporarily threatens Dubno from the southwest. This would have been very undesirable in view of the large dumps at Dubno." (Halder, 181).

A panzer division

After initial success, the Soviet attacks bogged down thanks to utter confusion among the commanders. Various parties issued orders and others countermanded them. The Germans recovered from their initially heavy losses and set about smashing their floundering opponents in detail. Luftwaffe Stuka dive-bombers devastated the Soviet armor in open country, destroying 201 tanks in one day alone. The Germans, their lighter tanks unable to easily destroy the heavy Soviet vehicles, used combined arms with antitank guns, artillery, and endless airstrikes to blow the Soviets to pieces.

As the Battle of Dubno reached its climax, the psychopathic Commissar Vashugin once more took a hand. Lieutenant General Dmitri Ryabyshev mustered the 8th Armored Corps on June 28th. He planned to attack on the 29th directly into Dubno, as soon as supporting units moved up. However, Commissar Vashugin arrived at Ryabyshev's field HQ on the road south of Dubno, already in a rage because the 8th was not advancing – despite this being the tactically sound choice.

Ryabyshev attempted to explain that he awaited more units to make a larger attack with flank support, rather than suicidally feeding his tanks in piecemeal. Another Commissar, Nikolai Popel, recorded the incredible scene which followed, though like many other men, he refused to name Vashugin in his memoirs, perhaps due to one of the many superstitions evinced by Russians: "[Vashugin] walked directly at Ryabyshev, trampling bushes with his highly polished boots. […] in a voice tense with fury, he asked, 'How much did you sell yourself for, Judas?' Ryabyshev was standing at […] attention in front of [Vashugin], confused, not knowing what to say […] Ryabyshev spoke up first: 'Comrade Corps Commissar, if you would hear me out...' 'You will be heard by military tribunal, traitor. Right here, under this fir, we'll hear you out, and right here we'll shoot you.'" (Kamenir, 2008, 205-206).

With his choices limited to a useless immediate assault or death by firing squad, Ryabyshev sent the 8th Motorized Corps into action without the supporting units that might have made the attack successful. He led his 303 tanks, including almost 100 T-34 and KV tanks, into the Battle of Dubno once again. Encountering the 16th Panzer Division, along with the German 57th and 75th Infantry Divisions, the 8th Motorized Corps recoiled after losing nearly 100 tanks, including over a dozen T-34s and 3 KV-1s.

At this point, Vashugin intervened, personally taking command and leading forward the 207 surviving tanks of the 8th Motorized Corps. The commissar, full of hubris but knowing nothing of actual combat, steered the tanks directly into a swamp. Vehicle after vehicle sank into the soft, muddy ground, brown water gurgling up to short out its engine and force its crew to abandon it. Only 43 tanks managed to pull back, leaving more than 150 destroyed by Vashugin's incompetence without a single German shot fired.

After this final disaster, Commissar Vashugin, suddenly overwhelmed with despair and probable guilt, shot himself. Khrushchev actually witnessed Vashugin's suicide, an action which undoubtedly brought great relief to all Soviet commanders in the Ukraine and might explain their somewhat improved performance thereafter. Khrushchev recalled, "[H]e said to me that he had decided to shoot himself. I said: 'What are you talking about? […]' He answered: 'I am guilty of giving incorrect orders to the commanders of the mechanized corps. I don't want to live any longer.' […] So I said: 'Why are you talking foolishness? If you've decided to shoot yourself, what are you waiting for?' I wanted to jolt him with some sharp words […] But he suddenly pulled out his pistol […], put it to his temple, fired, and fell." (Khrushchev, 2005, 310).

With the Soviet armor utterly smashed at the Battle of Dubno, the Germans secured the large, welcome fuel depots in the town, then moved on towards the Dniester. The Soviets knocked out some 200 German tanks in the battle, but of these, the Germans wrote off only 25, the remainder repaired and soon put back into service. The Soviets, by contrast, lost a minimum of 800 tanks, the vast majority lost behind German lines and therefore irretrievable.

Army Group South had won free operational space and could continue the offensive rapidly on its own terms. Ahead lay the Stalin Line, a defensive line anchored on the Pripet Marshes in the north, and beyond that, the city of Kiev, the Dnieper River, and the industrial Donbas region, all, as it seemed, ripe for the plucking.

Chapter 3: The Fighting Outside of Kiev

Picture of a German soldier passing a destroyed tank and a dead crew member in Ukraine

Even as the Germans were hurtling units east at the start of the invasion, commissar Nikita Khrushchev assisted in directing the effort to build up defensive works around Kiev. The task proved particularly challenging. The Irpin River, meandering just to the west of Kiev, resembles a mere brook compared to the mighty Dnieper, but presented a formidable obstacle to mechanized forces in 1941 due to the swamps and marshes of its floodplain.

The Soviets built a Kiev defensive belt along the Irpin in the late 1920s, completing it in 1930. However, Khrushchev found this in complete disrepair thanks to an order from Stalin: "There were reinforced concrete pillboxes with artillery there, but I have already mentioned how they were destroyed [...] Stalin ordered them destroyed. His intention [...] was that our command staff would not look back, but would keep its eyes fixed on the fortifications along our new border [...] Some reinforced concrete structures still existed, but there were no weapons in them [...]

[We] began gathering together anything we could: rifles, cannon, and so on, with the aim of building up a defensive line somehow (Khrushchev, 2005, 315).

The Soviet 26th Army under Lieutenant General Fyodor Yakovlevich Kostenko worked on the new defensive works, while Khrushchev mobilized and organized 160,000 civilians from Kiev to assist. Working feverishly, the Ukrainians completed an impressive defensive zone in a surprisingly brief time. By the time the Germans arrived, 18 miles of antitank trenches defended the approaches to Kiev, along with 750 new concrete or log bunkers and vast swathes of barbed wire entanglements.

This impressive effort, restoring and even augmenting the original defenses, soon bore fruit. The first direct move against Kiev occurred on July 10th, when III Panzer Corps under Friedrich von Mackensen made a rapid drive directly towards the city. However, when Mackensen arrived at the Irpin, he declined to attack without infantry support (100 miles to the rear), not wishing to risk his valuable panzers in a frontal assault on a fortified, well-defended metropolis. Though the Irpin itself represented a trivial obstacle, the soft ground and swamps flanking it represented a fatally dangerous zone for armor to attempt traversing while under fire from a dense concentration of bunkers.

Khrushchev's efforts had already bought time for the defenders and citizens of Kiev. Nevertheless, the 13th and 14th Panzer Divisions and the 25th Motorized Infantry Division loomed threateningly on the Irpin's west bank for days, foreshadowing the Germans' determination to take Kiev.

On July 10th, despite the appearance of Mackensen near Kiev, Kirponos launched an attack southeast against Panzer Group I's flank near Berdychev. German Panzerjäger I tank destroyers – gimmicky modifications of the Panzer I tank with an open fighting compartment housing a 4.7 cm PaK(t) antitank gun – of Abteilung 670 had already mauled the 5th Army's tank assets near Zhitomir two days previously.

The Soviets attacked with desperate courage, committing the 9th, 19th, and 22nd Mechanized Corps against Kleist's divisions, supported by three rifle corps and all the aircraft the Soviets could still muster. Under the blazing Ukrainian summer sun, the Germans and Soviets maneuvered, fought, and died on the flat landscape, cut by riverbeds and dotted with villages, in a ferocious combat lasting nearly four days. When the three Mechanized Corps withdrew late on July 13th, only 95 tanks remained between them. III Panzer Corps shifted away from Kiev as the German 6th Aarmy's infantry finally caught up with their armor's dashing advance, and Kleist, with Panzer Group I now reassembled and the Soviet 5th Army on the retreat, decided to strike rapidly between the 5th Army and the Soviet 6th and 12th Armies to the south of Kiev.

Hitler, watching the unfolding situation of all three Army Groups in detail, issued Fuhrer Directive No. 33 on July 19th, 1941. This directive fell in perfectly with Kleist's inclinations, reading in part that "the most important object is, by concentric attacks, to destroy the enemy 12th and 6th Armies while they are still west of the Dnieper." (Forczyk, 2013, 93-94).

The situation near Kiev now took an even more disastrous turn, if possible, for the Soviets. The Stavka (Soviet supreme command) formed the 5th Cavalry Corps and 4th Rifle Corps, located east of the Dnieper, into the Soviet 26th Army, then threw this across to the river's west bank, south of Kiev, in an effort to help the 6th and 12th Armies.

Kleist devised a bold operational plan to effect the destruction of the targeted Soviet armies. He sent Mackensen's III Panzer Corps east to halt the Soviet 26th Army at the Dnieper, while the infantry of the German 6th Army continued to invest Kiev despite heavy artillery fire from the defenders. The XIV and XLVIII Panzer Corps made a swift encircling movement around the Soviet 6th and 12th Armies on the eastern side, while infantry divisions of the German 17th Army advanced from the west, acting as the hammer crushing the Soviets against the anvil of the XIV and XLVIII Panzer Corps.

As frequently happens in war, Kleist's plan did not survive contact with the enemy, but the Battle of Uman, or the Uman Encirclement, nevertheless developed into a catastrophic loss for the Soviets. Mackensen's III Panzer Corps, including the SS Wiking Division, surged eastward against the Soviet 26th Army's 10 divisions on July 15th. Simultaneously, Werner Kempf's XLVIII Panzer Corps pushed south and west, driving the Soviet 6th Army westwards toward the relentlessly advancing German 17th Army. The XIV Panzer Corps drove into the gap between the 6th and 26th Armies, increasing the isolation of the two Soviet armies in the Uman pocket. On July 18th, the XIV Panzer Corps swung east to help Mackensen's III Panzer Corps against the 26th Army.

The battle raged on throughout late July. Kempf's panzers in the east and the 17th Army infantry in the west, led by Karl-Heinrich von Stulpnagel, slowly tightened their encirclement. This gradually closed the remaining gap in the southeast through which the Soviets might have escaped, but Stalin's order to retreat only straight eastward was an impossible maneuver thanks to the dense masses of aggressive German panzer divisions in the way.

A panzer division

The Soviets nevertheless fought hard, surprising the Germans with the savagery of their resistance. General-Major Yuri Novoselsky led the Soviet 2nd and 24th Motorized Corps, the former mustering one KV-1 and 18 T-34 tanks alongside the T-26 light tanks still comprising the bulk of the Red Army's armor, to block the 11th and 16th Panzer Divisions.

Meeting at Monastryshchye on July 21st, the Soviet and German forces struggled in a desperate week-long battle which kept the pocket from closing immediately. This fight continued until July 27th, when loss of tanks and lack of fuel to run the remaining armored vehicles obliged Novoselsky to abandon the attack. The Soviet 18th Army attempted to intervene, but only succeeded in allowing the Germans to trap part of its manpower in the Uman Pocket also.

The German 17th Army continued its relentless advance, using the Hungarian troops of Major General Bela Miklos to conduct local mobile operations as needed. Though the 17th technically represented an infantry army, the Hungarian Rapid Corps, with slightly more than divisional strength, fielded three battalions of 38M Toldi light tanks, four motorized infantry battalions, and twice as many bicycle battalions! Despite the eccentric forces under his command, Miklos proved an able, aggressive, decisive leader.

Miklos

The leading elements of the 17th Army and the SS Leibstandarte linked up at Pervomaysk's bridge across the Bug River on August 2nd, completing the encirclement of the Soviet 6th, 12th, and part of the 18th Armies at Uman, south of Kiev. Miklos' Rapid Corps and the 9th Panzer Division met on August 3rd, strengthening the girdle of men and machines now hemming in 20 divisions of Red Army soldiers. The Germans now set about squeezing the pocket, compressing it from all sides and pounding it with artillery. The thundering barrages, creeping forward ahead of the advancing Wehrmacht and directed at concentrations of Soviet troops gathering for a breakout attempt, smashed tanks, trucks, and men with lethal impartiality.

By August 5th, the remaining Soviets found themselves packed into an area consisting of only

14 square miles. In the process, the Germans hammered the Uman Pocket with more artillery shells than they had used during the entire invasion of France, Scandinavia, and the Low Countries combined.

Finally, on August 8th, the despairing Soviets stopped fighting, permitting the Germans to round them up in vast numbers. The generals of the 6th and 12th Armies, Ivan Muzychenko and Pavel Ponyedelin, surrendered to the Germans and spent the rest of the war at the Bavarian POW camp Stalag VII-A. Liberated by the US 14th Armored Division on April 29th, 1945, the two men returned to the USSR. While Muzychenko lived out the rest of his life, Stalin ordered Ponvedelin shot in 1950.

The German OKW's final report on the Uman Encirclement described the outcome: "German troops, in cooperation with Hungarian formations, have enjoyed great success in the Ukraine [...] Over 103,000 prisoners [...] have fallen into our hands. 317 tanks, 858 guns, 242 anti-tank cannons and air defense guns, 5,250 trucks, twelve railroad trains, and additional war materials have been captured. Enemy losses total more than 200,000 men." (Haupt, 1998, 39).

Those men who escaped the trap almost all fled to the port city of Odessa, where they soon found themselves encircled anew, either to be taken prisoner or be evacuated by sea. The Germans paid for their victory with 4,610 killed and 15,458 wounded, a casualty ratio of 10:1 in their favor. This indicated the difficulty of the fighting, since elsewhere during Barbarossa the Germans inflicted losses at a rate of 20:1 or even 30:1.

Chapter 4: Initial Assaults on Kiev

In the wake of that fighting, the German 17th Army next advanced toward the Dnieper, pushing the Soviet units on the western bank back to the river. The 11th Army joined them, while Kleist sent Panzer Group I south to occupy the remaining territory between Kiev, the Dnieper, and the sea. The Soviets, hard-pressed by the relentless panzer divisions, used large numbers of antitank mines for the first time, inflicting some damage on their pursuers and slowing the pursuit, even as the eventual result remained a foregone conclusion.

While the Germans mopped up the western bank of the Dnieper, Kirponos, defending Kiev with Vlasov's 37th Army and the Soviet 5th Army under another skilled soldier, Lieutenant General Mikhail Potapov, did not remain wholly idle. Though lacking armor, with only around three dozen tanks still operational, Kirponos flung these against Malyn, just northwest of Kiev, on July 24th, supported by one division of cavalry and two rifle (infantry) divisions.

The Wehrmacht LI Army Corps held Malyn, anchoring the left (northern) flank of the German 6th Army, investing Kiev from the west and facing Khrushchev's bunkers and defensive works across the swampy Irpin River. The LI Army Corps flung the Russians back, but Kirponos fed more reinforcements in, with attacks continuing against the 6th Army flank for 12 days, with the last occurring on August 4th.

Once Kirponos' 5th Army recoiled, leaving the landscape around Malyn strewn with burned out Russian vehicles and windrows of Soviet corpses, the German 6th Army attempted the first serious assault against Kiev. Their commanders hoped that the Russians had depleted their forces sufficiently during the nearly two-week Malyn battle to crumple under the assault of a single German army.

General Hans von Obstfelder, then 55 years of age but destined to live to 90 and be decorated with the Knight's Cross of the Iron Cross with Oak Leaves and Swords for bravery, led his XXIX Army Corps forward across the Irpin River against Khrushchev's defensive works on August 8th. Six infantry divisions – the 44th, 71st, 75th, 95th, 99th, and 299th – rolled against the Soviet defensive belt, but found it manned and powerful: "The regiments were literally 'devoured' by forests, fire, and fanatic Russian soldiers. After four days of bloody combat, they could not force a breakthrough in the fortified positions. The commander of the 6th Army suspended the battle. The 6th Army now stood at order arms." (Haupt, 1998, 57-58).

Obstfelder

While Kirponos and the German 5th Army exchanged ineffective but costly blows, the Germans continued pushing south and east, conquering the Ukraine west of the Dnieper. The crucial turning point arrived when Stalin authorized the Soviet 5th Army elements seeking to impede this advance to fall back behind the wide river on August 16th.

By August 19th, the Germans controlled all the territory up to the Dnieper. Since the river turns southeast at Kiev and flows in that direction all the way to Dnepropetrovsk, where it turns south again, this actually enabled German forces to occupy territory far east of Kiev. Even before the Wehrmacht forced the crossings that remained intact, this placed Kiev at the point of a large, triangular salient projecting out into German-held areas. Army Group Center outflanked this salient to some degree to the north, and Gerd von Rundstedt's Army Group South lay along its southern flank. This naturally suggested pinching off the salient, and the vast numbers of men it contained, via a double envelopment far east of Kiev, with one force driving from the north and the other from the south to pinch off the salient as a huge pocket. This would necessarily force the surrender or annihilation of the men trapped within.

The plan now adopted by Hitler in fact followed exactly this pattern. The Soviet commanders on the ground were keenly aware of the possibility, but they did not dare to retreat without express orders from Stalin. The records of Soviet military action are peppered with the summary executions of Red Army generals who "retreated," even if only for the sake of prudent tactic maneuver, so the fears of Kirponos and the other men leading the Kiev defensive forces represented realism instead of paranoid overcautiousness.

Even Khrushchev, who in his memoirs frankly admitted to ordering the execution of soldiers who fell back in the face of overwhelming German attacks and prompting a junior officer's suicide, realized the perilous situation. He and Budyonny conferred about how to deal with a German encircling movement from the south, possibly hindering it long enough for the hundreds of thousands of men in the salient to escape: "After considerable thought we arrived at the following decision: to take a certain number of troops and artillery and cover our flank in the direction from Kiev toward Kremenchug, so that there, in the Ukrainian steppe, there would be something with which to block the enemy's path northward and not allow him to close the ring of encirclement. What could we take? It was obvious that the troops we had in Kiev were so far not being used. The situation there was quiet, and the enemy was making no moves against Kiev." (Khrushchev, 2005, 341).

Budyonny

The Marshal and the commissar prepared the orders and sent them to Moscow for approval. However, even withdrawing troops from Kiev to guard the salient's flank resembled a retreat too much for the Soviet Union's dictator to countenance it. Neither Stalin nor the Stavka issued any direct reply to the requested orders; instead, an aircraft arrived carrying Marshal Semyon Timoshenko, and orders for Budyonny to hand over command to the newcomer immediately.

Timoshenko

Timoshenko toured the salient and Kiev with Khrushchev. Possessing enough military acumen to correctly assess the situation, he agreed with Khrushchev that disaster loomed. However, nothing could be done, since Stalin would not hesitate to shoot any officer, even a Marshal of the Soviet Union, who ordered a retreat without his authorization – an authorization neither Timoshenko nor Khrushchev could secure.

Thus, vast hordes of Red Army soldiers awaited their doom inside the Kiev salient or the city itself, and the Germans busied themselves preparing to take this effectively sacrificial force in the iron jaws of yet another vast pocket. On September 15th, General Gotthard Heinrici wrote to his family, marveling over the Soviet failure to retreat from the trap. Of course, at that time he knew nothing of Stalin's orders: "We are just about to encircle the Russian. All troops west of Kiev will bite the dust. For some reason I cannot comprehend, the Russian has assigned his troops in the Ukraine in a way that invites us to take them all prisoners. The encirclement is getting tighter. [...] We already fight for the roads that will be essential for the enemy's retreats. While I am writing this I can hear artillery fire rolling continuously." (Hurter, 2014, 83). The incomprehensible reason, of course, resided in the deeply unmilitary but extremely meddlesome mind of Stalin. Both he and Hitler fancied themselves great generals of the caliber of Alexander the Great, Napoleon, and Gustavus Adolphus, even as they were bringing millions of their own soldiers to grief through incompetent intervention.

The wide flow of the Dnieper, approximately half a mile wide below Kiev and averaging 25 feet deep, represented a formidable obstacle that both men and vehicles required bridges to cross. The Soviets, once forced back to the eastern bank, demolished many of the existing bridges. Nevertheless, some fell into German hands, including those overlooked, those taken by daring attacks before demolition occurred, or those damaged but not destroyed and therefore fairly easy to repair.

A picture of German engineers constructing a pontoon bridge across the Dnieper

At Dnepropetrovsk, the Soviets destroyed the bridges but built a pontoon bridge to allow their own retreat once ousted from the city. However, when the Red Army engineers set off the charges on the pontoon bridge, they managed to damage it but did not break it up. The unsteady span remaining offered enough continuous surface for infantry to cross, but not vehicles. Thus, the 13th Panzer Division sent dismounted panzergrenadiers across on August 25th to establish a beachhead on the far bank, then moved engineers onto the pontoon bridge to repair it. Within a few days, the Germans restored the Soviet structure to full strength, enabling panzers, halftracks, and trucks with towed artillery to cross. The Wiking SS Panzer Division under SS-Brigadefuhrer Felix Steiner crossed on September 2nd,, indicating the engineers rendered the bridge suitable for heavy armor by that date.

Other bridges fell into German hands in a more dramatic fashion. When Stalin allowed the Soviet 5th Army to fall back to the Dnieper's east bank, those units which earlier attacked Malyn retreated through Gornostaipel to 1.8 mile long wooden bridge north of Kiev at a particularly wide part of the river. Today, the site is flooded by a large reservoir. At the time, this bridge spanned the river, connecting the banks with a large inhabited island in the middle.

The retreating 5th Army troops failed to blow up this bridge. On August 23rd at 7 PM, infantry from the German 111th Infantry Division and StuG III Sturmgeschutz self-propelled assault guns of Sturmartillerie-Abteilung 191 attacked the still-intact span. First, two StuG IIIs drove at speed onto the bridge, hoping to take it swiftly. However, one of the SPGs rolled off the edge of the bridge and plunged into the river below as it tried to maneuver around an abandoned Soviet truck, and the second StuG III retreated.

Undeterred, the Germans launched a fresh attack, led by Leutnant Kurt-Heinz Bingler in a StuG III. Infantry, some of them manhandling wheeled antitank guns forward at speed, and engineers followed. The engineers successfully cut the ignition cables to the Soviet explosives in place on the bridge before the defenders on the far bank could set off the demolition charges. Major Friedrich Musculus described the action: "The enemy dominated the bridge with anti-tank guns and machine-guns from 12 bunkers on the opposite eastern bank. […] The enemy bunkers […] were engaged with high explosives and machine-guns from all sides, and this blocked the view from their portholes. […] Once again, Lieutenant Bingler took up the lead with an assault gun. […] The assault troops reached the eastern bank with modest losses, enemy fire was erratic, and the Russian bunkers were captured in hand-to-hand combat." (Haupt, 1998, 61-62),

The drama of the Gornostaipel bridge had not yet reached its conclusion, however. Kirponos, receiving reports that the Germans captured the bridge intact, sent the bombers still available to him to attack it. These aircraft succeeded in partially collapsing areas of the wooden span, temporarily isolating 25th Motorized Infantry Division infantry on the midstream island. Nonetheless, these men found their temporary island prison something of a paradise. The bombs killed a number of fish, which the Germans retrieved, cooked, and ate, When these ran out, they went fishing successfully with hand grenades. The inhabitants had also planted numerous crops, now ripe and ready to eat, including yellow melons, grapes, tomatoes, and apricots. The men also frequently went swimming in the river.

While the Germans were enjoying this seemingly idyllic reprieve, Khrushchev had arranged for a number of gunboats to patrol the river as monitors. These Soviet river monitors interrupted the 25th Division soldiers' leisurely activities, putting troops ashore in an effort to take the island and, presumably, complete the destruction of the bridge, as Erwin Boehm later recalled: "During the morning, the Russians suddenly attacked the island. They approached the southern end in large [monitors]. We laid down heavy fire and sank two […] In spite of this, the Russians were able to get a foothold. […] a great number of them […] were now attempting to overrun our beautiful island from the south. We had to abandon our defensive positions and establish new ones further to the rear." (Haupt, 1998, 58).

The Germans landed reinforcements on the island with their own assault boats and managed to oust the Soviets from it. In the following days, the Wehrmacht's engineers busily repaired the Gornostaipel span, making it ready to play its part in the coming envelopment battle and destruction of the Soviet 5th Army.

In other areas, the Germans used boats to cross the river, establishing beachheads on the eastern shore. Gottlob Bidermann of the 132nd Infantry Division described one such crossing just north of Kanev, a city fiercely held by the Soviets for some time before they withdrew to the eastern bank or surrendered. The 132nd put soldiers across the river at Kodoriv, supporting them by artillery fire from the town of Kodoriv itself.

The Soviets counterattacked the 132nd's beachhead repeatedly, but the Germans beat them off, pushing more and more units across the river and driving inland as their strength permitted. Bidermann recounted a series of counterattacks defeated one night after dark: "The night suddenly exploded with impacting artillery rounds – and along the […] road in the northwest area […] eleven enemy attacks were repulsed between the hours of 2210 and 0250. The sunrise bore witness to the effectiveness of our defense, as countless bodies clad in khaki-brown could be seen lying in heaps before our positions. Burning vehicles littered the landscape, sending plumes of oily black smoke skyward (Bidermann, 2000, 44-45).

Army Group South's Gerd von Rundstedt continued pushing men and machines across the Dnieper at multiple points, building up a formidable array of units on the eastern shore. For the moment, these units mostly built up, only attacking to expand and improve their positions. The plan now involved waiting for the arrival of Heinz Guderian's Panzer Group II from the north, dispatched by Hitler from Army Group Center to complete the Kiev encirclement.

The Soviets continued large numbers of attacks on the Germans during this period, trying to push them back and possibly regain a foothold on the Dnieper's western bank. However, the tough Wehrmacht and SS professionals shredded these assaults, made by courageous but poorly trained, equipped, and led Red Army soldiers who often lacked sufficient rifles to fully outfit their units.

Chapter 5: The Arrival of Guderian

With Smolensk taken and the rail lines laid to logistically support a forward leap to Moscow, Hitler changed his plans abruptly in August, stopping the drive on the Russian capital and instead turning Guderian's panzers toward Kiev. The panzer general met with Hitler in person at the Wolfsschanze ("Wolf's Lair") in Rastenburg, Prussia, arguing in detail for a continued Moscow advance while good weather lasted, but the Fuhrer would have none of it, even as he allowed Guderian to fully express his views. Hitler then detailed his reasoning and stated his generals did not know how to run a war, a theme he would return to repeatedly, and often wildly inaccurately.

Hitler and Goering at the Wolf's Lair

Guderian did, however, secure one minor victory. Hitler's original plan called for leaving part of Panzer Group II with Army Group Center, and using another portion to attack towards Kiev. The panzer general managed to persuade the Fuhrer to let him keep his unit intact and use its entire force for the Kiev expedition. Guderian hoped this would shorten the operation, perhaps leaving enough time to strike at Moscow prior to winter.

"Hammering Heinz" flew back from Fuhrer headquarters to Panzer Group II on August 22nd, reaching his lodgings early the following morning. After snatching a few hours' sleep, the general received OKH orders: "The object is to destroy as much of the strength of the Russian Fifth Army as possible, and to open the Dneiper crossings for Army Group South with maximum speed. For this purpose a strong force, preferably commanded by Colonel-General Guderian, is to move forward, with its right wing directed on Chernigov." (Guderian, 1996, 202).

Guderian's Panzer Group II moved south from Gomel, their maneuver hindered by water obstacles and other rough terrain. In doing so, Guderian found himself with Soviet forces on both sides of his advance. Defeated but still cohesive Soviet units to the west attempted to push east, escaping from the Gomel area back to Red Army lines.

The XXIV Panzer Corps, under a general with the resounding name of Leo Dietrich Franz Geyr von Schweppenburg, received the difficult task of simultaneously attacking south and guarding Panzer Group II's right (western) flank. On the left flank, Soviet forces massed beyond the Sudost River, a tributary of the Desna. With the Sudost very low due to summer drought, Guderian recognized it as a trivial obstacle to the Red Army, assigning XLVII Panzer Corps under Joachim Lemelsen to guard this flank.

In response, Kirponos, clearly aware of Guderian's advance within hours of its commencement, found himself obliged to disperse his forces even more, facing some south and southwest in anticipation of Army Group South's northward pincer and aligning others along the Desna River to form the northern flank of the salient against Guderian's advance.

Considerable fighting took place on the southward drive, but the Soviet units proved disorganized, confused, and lacking in mobility thanks to the logistical stranglehold of German railway seizures cutting off their gasoline supply. Stavka formed two new armies, the 37th Army and the 40th Army under Kuzma Podlas, later killed near Kharkov. With supporting units falling back or fleeing and low quality recruits making up much of their force, these armies failed to do more than provide a temporary obstacle that Guderian brushed aside with ease.

Leading units of Guderian's hard-hitting Panzer Group I reached the Desna River within two days, seizing a number of bridges intact, possibly due to Soviet expectations of a slower advance. In other places, Wehrmacht engineers threw pontoon bridges across the winding Ukrainian river to allow units to pass over to the south bank.

Audacious, abrasive, and willing to stand up even to Hitler on military matters, Walter Model drove his 3rd Panzer Division south to Novgorod-Severskyi, where a major wooden road bridge crosses the Desna. At this point, the confluence of the Desna and Vit Rivers forms a "braided" flow, with an entangled profusion of channels forming scores of low-lying-marshy islands. The road bridge crosses both rivers and one of the largest of the islands at the eastern extremity of Novgorod-Severskyi, stretching no less than 2,400 feet. The Soviets had prepared the bridge for demolition, wiring a 500 pound bomb at its center (Kirchubel, 2003, 56), hanging explosives from its sides in green rubber bags, and suspending drums of gasoline from the upper wooden superstructure to complete the conflagration. Model, however, surprised the Soviets; the leading elements consisted of motorcycle troops in the extremely rugged Zundapp KS750, a motorcycle whose features included a locking differential for equally effective on-road and off-road use, 751cc motor, hydraulic brakes, a 10-gear transmission system, a high-mounted carburetor intake providing operability in deep mud or during fording, and a sidecar with a powered wheel and pintle-mounted MG34 machine gun. Immediately behind them came armored SdKfz 251 halftracks packed full of panzergrenadiers, plus engineers to disable the demolitions on the bridge. Ernst-Georg Buchterkirch, who had led the successful capture of several bridges across the Seine during the Invasion of France and personally knocked out six French tanks as commander of a Panzer, now led this attack also.

Model

Guderian summarized the results briefly but enthusiastically in his memoirs: "On my way there I received a surprising and most gratifying signal: by brilliant employment of his tanks Lieutenant Buchterkirch (of the 6th Panzer Regiment of the 3rd Panzer Division) had managed to capture the 750-yard bridge over the Desna to the east of Novgorod-Severskie intact. This stroke of good fortune should make our future operations considerably less difficult." (Guderian, 1996, 206).

Though the lack of demolition represented sheer "good fortune," as Guderian stated, the rest of the operation hinged on military skill. Artillery preparation began at 6:00 a.m. and continued for two hours, after which the motorcycle troops on their Zundapp KS750s roared forward at speed onto the bridge, engaging the Soviets in a frantic firefight with their MG34 machine guns. The

Soviets returned a heavy fire, wrecking motorcycles and killing and wounding men as they raced along the span.

The German artillery dropped smoke shells on the bridge. With a sharp clattering of treads, SdKfz 251 halftracks loomed suddenly out of the gray pall, their sleek, faceted hulls suddenly disgorging squads of panzergrenadiers. Pioneers moved just behind the halftracks, snipping detonation wires on the Soviet explosives. These men cut the ropes suspending the fuel drums from the wooden superstructure, then rolled the incendiary barrels over the bridge's side into the Desna.

Determined Soviet sappers clambered along the underside of the bridge, hanging on to wooden beams and joists. However, Panzer III tanks lined up along the German shore spotted them, directing a hail of machine gun fire at the human figures scrambling underneath the span. Dead and dying men dropped from the structure to send up fountains of spray from the Desna or Vit surface. The sappers nevertheless started several fires, which the Wehrmacht pioneers promptly extinguished.

After a desperate fight, the Soivets fell back from the bridge, leaving it in German hands. Nearby Soviet batteries opened fire with high explosive rounds, hoping to blow the bridge to matchwood, but their aim proved poor, and though the area rocked under the impact of shells, not one struck the bridge itself. The assault began at 8:00 and had succeeded by 8:30. By 9:00 a.m., the Germans cleared the bridge of wrecks, bodies, and debris, and the full stream of the 3rd Panzer Division's armor began flowing across.

On September 6th, elements of the SS Division "Das Reich" seized another Desna bridge in spectacular fashion. A battalion-strength unit of motorcycle troops, equipped with tough BMW and Zundapp motorcycles fitted with sidecars armed with pintle-mounted MG34 machine guns, the regiment "Der Fuhrer," plus engineers, raced ahead of the main division to cut off retreating Soviet troops.

As this ad hoc raiding party reached Sosnitsa, fresh orders arrived. Scouts had located an undamaged railway bridge at Makoshyno on the Desna River and the men received the command to seize this valuable asset. Arriving at the riverbank just west of a bend in the river, where the iron trestle bridge still stands in the early 21st century, the Germans awaited promised Stuka bomber support at 1:30 PM.

When 2:30 p.m. arrived with no sign of the Stukas, Guderian, who arrived in person on the scene, ordered the attack anyway. "The motor-cycle assault opened. At full speed the machines were raced over the sleepers and before the Russians could react […] the leading SS groups, whose machine-gunners in the side-cars sprayed the area with bursts of fire, had smashed through the enemy barricades. Behind the SS battalion Army engineers moved slowly cutting detonation wires […] and taking away the high explosive charges." (Lucas, 1991, 66).

SS-Sturmbannfuhrer Fritz Rentrop received the Knight's Cross of the Iron Cross for leading this attack. The bridge fell intact into German hands, providing yet another important crossing of the Desna, which was 400 feet wide at this point. Ironically, the Stukas arrived late, 27-strong, and dive-bombed the victorious SS motorcycle troops, killing 10 and wounding almost 30, thereby inflicting far more casualties with friendly fire than had the hostile fire of the surprised Soviet defenders.

In this and a number of similar actions, Panzer Group II secured a number of crossings along the length of the Desna. This galvanized the Soviet armies, nearly prostrate in recent days, to a fresh burst of activity in an effort to drive the Germans back. In some cases, they actually succeeded temporarily, though the arrival of new units eventually crushed their efforts: "By August 31st, [...] The 10th (Motorized) Infantry Division succeeded in crossing the Desna, to the north of Korop, but was thrown back again to the west bank by heavy Russian counterattacks, besides being attacked on its right flank by strong enemy forces. By sending in the very last man of the division, in this case the Field Bakery Company, a catastrophe to the right flank was only just avoided." (Guderian, 1996, 208).

Though the Red Army put up a desperate final defense of the river line, knowing clearly that the movement of significant German forces to their bank spelled the end of the Kiev salient, the Germans could not be stopped. Guderian requested and received another panzer corps, the XLVI Panzer Corps, giving him an even more potent striking force to execute his mission.

Panzer and infantry divisions poured across the Desna from the north in early September, massing like a gathering avalanche on the northern flank of the Kiev salient. With Panzer Group I and other Army Group South elements present in powerful bridgeheads on the east bank of the Dnieper, the Germans found themselves poised to deliver the coup de grace to their enemies, trapped in place by Stalin's orders.

Chapter 6: The Encirclement and Fall of Kiev

Guderian at a command post near Kiev during the battle

The start of September brought heavy periodic rains to the Ukrainian grasslands. This signaled the start of the autumn rasputitsa, the wet season that turns Russian roads into nearly bottomless quagmires of sucking mud. A second rasputitsa occurred with the spring rains and snow melt, but the autumn version of this phenomenon proved especially grim.

Nevertheless, the Wehrmacht prepared to carry out their attack with full vigor and planning, particularly on the days without rain, when hot, sunny weather still managed to rapidly dry the roads again. On September 2nd, Field Marshal Albert Kesselring, commander of the regional air operations, flew from Army Group South's headquarters to Guderian's field HQ to confirm that German forces occupied the east bank of the Dnieper and that they stood ready for cooperative operations.

The Soviets, finding their ground forces baffled for lack of armor support, turned to raids by Ilyushin DB-3 twin-engined tactical bombers, first manufactured in 1935. Though the crews showed considerable courage in braving the whirlwind of German flak, the rather obsolete bombers inflicted only very light damage, failing to hamper the Wehrmacht buildup on either flank of the salient.

Panzer Group II continued probing for a weak point throughout the first week of September.

The Russians, though unable to maneuver enough for notable counterattacks, resisted stubbornly wherever possible, clearly aware of the stakes involved. Finally, on September 9th, Walter Model's 3rd Panzer Division found a weak link in the Soviet lines. Attacking with great élan despite the wretched weather conditions and a moderately alarming fuel situation, Model's men punched easily through the detected gap and sped south towards the next objective of Romny.

The plan now called for Guderian to break through to Romny, while Kleist would strike north towards Lubny, directly south of Romny. The forces would then link up somewhere near Lochvitsa, midway between Romny and Lubny, sealing the pocket and the doom of the men inside it.

This, of course, only represented the easternmost limit of the double envelopment. West of this point, units would drive north and south into the trapped Russians, chopping the pocket into smaller pockets that could subsequently be isolated, compressed, and eventually eliminated. Turning the larger pocket into a honeycomb of smaller pockets prevented the Soviets from mustering a force anywhere that would be large enough to break the envelopment itself.

On the 10th of September, Guderian attempted to accompany Model's drive to Romny, but he arrived only hours after the town fell due to the appallingly muddy roads. Model's men took Romny by surprise, overwhelming the Russians before they could man its strong defensive belts. However, snipers remained at large in the town, hiding in the walled gardens, so the Germans moved about in halftracks or not at all.

At 5 p.m., with the XLVI Panzer Corps arriving – including the SS Panzer Division "Das Reich" – Model conducted a detailed sweep of the town, which killed or captured all the remaining snipers or drove them out into the rain-lashed countryside. One of the Das Reich soldiers noted both the unexpected advantages and expected downsides of the rain: "At 02:00 hours rations came up. At last something hot to eat and enough bread. We advance along the side of the railway line and the Russian shells sink into the swamp which we are crossing and do not usually explode. […] It is very tiring walking on the sleepers. […] Our feet are suffering from being continually wet from the rain and the swamp." (Lucas, 1991, 67).

On September 9th, Kleist established another crucial bridgehead over the Dneiper. Near Kremenchug, the 257th Infantry Division under Lieutenant General Sachs conducted a "wild assault" using 150 rafts and 68 assault boats. Once they forced the river, the engineers quickly built a 650 foot long combat bridge capable of supporting heavy armor.

The 9th, 13th, and 16th Panzer Divisions crossed this pontoon bridge on the night of 11th to 12th September during an intense rainstorm that rendered the blackness over the wide river complete. Two motorized infantry divisions followed, enabling a huge force of 5 divisions to mass on the bank in preparation for attack.

Under an overcast sky at the first light of dawn, these five divisions punched north behind a rolling artillery barrage, crashing headlong into the Soviet 38th Army under Major General Nikolai Feklenko. The unexpected attack shattered the Soviet formation, leading to a rout that had the Soviets fleeing their field fortifications. Feklenko himself only escaped his farmhouse headquarters by leaping out a window at the back as Panzergrenadiers burst in the front door and killed or captured many members of his staff.

The onrush of the three leading panzer divisions pierced 40 miles forward towards Lubny in the first day alone, capturing 13,000 Russians in the process, besides destroying 75 tanks. The infantry divisions only advanced 12 miles, but nevertheless continued their dogged march in the wake of the panzers.

The 16th Panzer Division rolled onward through the night, reaching the Sula River early on September 13th, some 72 miles from the unit's starting position at daybreak the day before. Under the dashing leadership of the superbly skilled Hans-Valentin Hube, known as "Der Mensch" and sporting a metal hand in place of the one shot away in combat at Aisne in 1914, the 16th Panzer Division hurled itself at Lubny but recoiled in the face of defenses manned by fanatical NKVD troops.

Kirponos, faced by the lethal advance of Panzer Group I from the south, ordered the Soviet 5th and 37th Armies to retreat north towards the Desna, where the German advance seemed slower. He flew out of the incipient pocket to Moscow in order to personally implore Stalin to permit him to withdraw as many men as possible from the trap, but the Soviet dictator refused. Knowing he would be executed if he disobeyed, Kirponos flew back to Kiev and resumed his command of the now hopeless defense.

Separately, Marshal Boris Shaposhnikov, the Deputy People's Commissar for Defense, and his protege Aleksandr Vasilevsky, made a last ditch effort to persuade Stalin of the necessity to save his soldiers from the grip of the Germans. Stalin authorized limited maneuvering by the 5th and 37th Armies: "In other words, this was a half-way measure. The mere mention of the urgent need to abandon Kiev threw Stalin into a rage and he momentarily lost his self-control. We evidently did not have sufficient will power to withstand these outbursts of uncontrollable rage or a proper appreciation of our responsibility for the impending catastrophe in the South-Western Direction." (Stahel, 2012, 173).

Shaposhnikov

Vasilevsky

After days of rain, the final push to close the pocket on September 14th occurred during superb, dry, sunny weather. Savoring this "panzer weather," Walter Model and his 3rd Panzer Division plunged south towards Lochvitsa. On the way, they encountered an enormous convoy of Soviet supply wagons and horse-drawn antitank artillery, guarded by a detachment of Cossack cavalry and two T-26 light tanks. The Germans immediately attacked, the panzers charging forward to strew destruction in the convoy with their machine guns and HE shells. The Russian drovers abandoned their draft animals and fled on foot, while the Cossacks kept up a brief firefight until the two light tanks "brewed up."

Having mopped up this group, the 3rd Panzer Division continued southward. Finally, they arrived at Lochvitsa, under attack by Hube "Der Mensch" and the 16th Panzer Division, who had arrived from the south: "It had been a while since the red-golden sun set. Finally, the combat group stopped on high ground and hid the vehicles behind scarecrows. The men looked over the silhouettes of the city through binoculars […] Clouds of smoke hung over the houses, and in between the crackle of machine guns the artillery hits thudded. There was no doubt […] a few kilometers further on were the lead elements of Army Group South." (Haupt, 1998, 75).

The leading panzer company rolled down the slope, scattering a group of Soviets who emerged from a ravine to fire briefly on the armored vehicles. Fording a brook, the leading elements of the 3rd Panzer Division rolled into Lochvitsa at approximately the same time as the leading tanks of the 16th Panzer Division. Guderian and Kleist had achieved the encirclement, penning hundreds of thousands of Red Army soldiers inside Kiev and a wedge of territory just east of it.

With the Soviets trapped, the Germans now needed to make good on their victory by capturing or killing the soldiers inside the Kiev pocket. The biggest danger lay in other Soviet forces from the east attacking the outer lines of encirclement to free their comrades. As it turned out, however, no such forces existed; the Red Army units nearby were weak and exhausted after having participated in the struggle to prevent the crossing of the Dnieper. Moreover, in anticipation of the threat against Moscow, the Soviet Stavka could not send any divisions south to aid Kirponos, let alone armies. In truth, the Soviet Union had – temporarily – run out of men. Those facing Army Group Center could not be moved for fear of exposing Moscow, while the Siberian divisions, though intact, lay at the far end of the country, much too far to be shifted in time to have the slightest effect on the outcome. With millions of men already dead, prisoners, or trapped in pockets, the USSR needed time to recruit and arm more before they could present any kind of threat to the Wehrmacht.

Throughout these dark days, Stalin continued to show a bold front, refusing to acknowledge the situation's hopelessness and describing fatalistic telegrams from the encircled commanders as "panicky." That said, it is likely he was afraid to admit his mistake and thus possibly invite his own toppling and execution, the fate that often befell a discredited dictator, and one remarkable action reveals that he in fact understood the magnitude of the disaster he engineered at Kiev. Despite his aversion to bringing any foreigners onto Russian soil, and his pathological paranoia about the hated West, the Soviet strongman sent a secret letter to British Prime Minister Winston Churchill. This letter read, in part, "If [...] a second front in the west seems unfeasible to the British government, then perhaps some other means could be found of rendering the Soviet Union active military aid against the common enemy. [...] Britain could safely land 25–30 divisions at Archangel or ship them to the southern areas of the USSR via Iran for military cooperation with the Soviet troops on Soviet soil." (Stahel, 2012, 225).

Sent on September 13th, this letter revealed the panic, possibly even terror, under Stalin's blustering surface. His suggestion that the British land in the south indicates a desperate fantasy of saving Kiev, an impossibility even had Churchill agreed right away, and it was indicative of a man feeling so trapped as to give way to self-delusion and wishful thinking.

Meanwhile, most of the Soviets streaming east from the disintegrating formations had only light weapons or none at all, and thus could not break out through the German cordon. In a few places, the dreadful KV-1 tanks appeared, leading groups of men trying to escape. In some cases, these vehicles actually managed to push through and escape eastward, while in others, the Germans used Stuka dive-bombers and 88mm flak guns used as direct fire antitank weapons to destroy them.

The Soviet 5th, 21st, 26th, and 37th Armies lay inside the Kiev pocket. As the operations to annihilate them began, the Luftwaffe flew over the "cauldron" with near impunity thanks to the destruction of all Soviet airfields inside the area. Cleverly, the German Stuka pilots looked for clumps of forest alongside major roads running through the pocket, dropping bombs among the tress. Though they usually could see nothing except treetops, the Luftwaffe men assumed that densely-packed groups of Russian men and vehicles likely sheltered there during the day, trying to hide from air attacks before continuing nighttime attempts at escape. Soviet eyewitness accounts indicate the efficacy of this tactic. While some bombs fell into unoccupied groves, many plunged directly into thickly concentrated Soviet units, blasting apart dozens of men and vehicles with every hit. In some cases, the use of incendiary bombs flushed Soviet units into the open, where the Germans strafed them relentlessly.

Staring defeat in the face, some of the Soviets turned to gruesome torture in revenge for their impending destruction. Eric Kemmeyer, an SS man, described one such scene, which was so ghastly the local German commander shot a large group of Soviet prisoners in response: "[I]n a small depression covered with apricot trees, was a small group of men whispering together. I pushed my way through them and shrank in horror [...] The small trees were bearing fruit, very strange fruit – German soldiers. They were not a pretty sight, with their arms tied high behind them to the weak branches, their jackboots off and their legs burnt and carbonized up to their knees. So distorted were their faces that even seasoned soldiers had to look away." (Stahl, 2010,

53-54). According to Kemmeyer, the Soviets had soaked the 102 prisoners' feet in gasoline, without getting the accelerant elsewhere on the men's bodies, and then set them afire. By burning the lower extremities, the men would eventually die from shock and generalized bleeding, but only after hours of excruciating agony – a method of execution dubbed "Stalin's socks."

More men preferred to surrender than to take such revenge, however, which only served to further inflame their already ruthless enemy. Nor could the Wehrmacht make their encirclement airtight, given the huge spaces involved and the unfamiliar terrain. Forests, river and stream beds, and darkness all gave cover for groups of Soviet soldiers or even individual men attempting to escape eastward.

The Germans caught many of these escapees nevertheless. The Wehrmacht troops took men in uniform prisoner, while those Red Army soldiers who discarded their telltale uniforms in favor of civilian clothes risked being hanged or shot as partisans if captured. In the end, approximately 15,000 soldiers eluded the Germans, rejoining their comrades in the east, while some 50 tanks broke out.

Some of the Soviets, unaware of the Germans' plans and deeply loathing the Soviet Union (with its own vast catalog of massacre, torture, engineered famine, and brutal political repression) actually sought to defect to the Germans rather than to escape the trap. One group of 200 men fought their way back to the Dnieper with submachine guns and grenades, killing the commissars who tried to stop them. Once they arrived at the Dnieper, they surrendered to the Germans. A Soviet soldier described the scene: "In our regiment, the division commissar gathered the privates and commanders and started to incite the people to get going, in order to force our way east. […] The Red Army soldiers became agitated. Our regimental commander called out to the privates: 'Who do you obey? Away with the damned Chekist!' The commissar instantly drew his revolver and shot. The commander fell down. Our second lieutenant and a group of Red Army soldiers jumped on the commissar – in less than a minute he was torn to pieces." (Berkhoff, 2004, 13).

Those who remained true to the Soviet Union's colors often found themselves under low-level but persistent sniper fire from the local inhabitants, who hoped to regain their national independence from the Soviet empire. Others, by contrast, received shelter, food, and other help from the local people, who attempted to help the escape the encirclement.

At army headquarters, General Franz Halder observed in rather colorful fashion that "enemy formations are bounding off the encirclement ring like billiard balls" (Stahel, 2012, 245). Soon enough, however, the Germans acted to stop even this futile activity. The LI Army Corps under Walter von Seydlitz-Kurzbach plunged south, cleaving the pocket in two and linking up with XXXIV Army Corps under General Alfred Wager, advancing north from the Dnieper. This junction occurred on September 18th.

On September 16, 1941, the German 71st and 296th Infantry Divisions spearheaded the attack by the XXIX Corps into Kiev proper (Kirchubel, 2003,66). The Germans fought their way forward through dense defensive works over the next three days, while the Soviet commissars attempted to bolster the defenders' morale by playing Stalin's speeches over numerous loudspeakers mounted throughout the defensive zone. A Wehrmacht eyewitness recorded the excitement the Germans felt at the sight of the city finally visible in the distance ahead of them: "Then a new tree-covered ridge rose, and beyond that, we could see what made our hearts beat faster: Kiev's characteristic towers rising clearly in the morning haze! […] To the right, we could make out the large iron bridge over the Dnepr, and behind it two additional bridges leading out of the center of the city." (Haupt, 1998, 80).

Encountering bunkers and dug-in Soviet tanks turned into quasi-pillboxes, the 95th Infantry Division worked to clear these obstacles. The 77th StuG III Battalion, made up of 21 Sturmgeschutz III assault guns, worked their way forward alongside the 95th, fulfilling their original role as anti-bunker weapons (later almost totally eclipsed by infantry support and tank hunting). These StuG IIIs still featured the short-barreled 7.5 cm KwK 37 L/24, useful in the cramped spaces of fortified sectors and urban areas, but later underwent upgrade to the 7.5 cm KwK 40 L/43 and soon the L/48, whose increased barrel length suited it better to anti-tank action.

The low, tough-looking StuG IIIs crawled forward through the maze of Soviet bunkers, the deep purring rumble of their engines punctuated by the crash of firing as they sent their shells punching through the concrete of enemy strongpoints. German infantry with demolition charges and flamethrowers also worked their way forward.

The assault guns likewise played an important role once the Germans penetrated into the streets of Kiev itself. The armored vehicles moved up to fire high explosive (HE) shells into any buildings held tenaciously by the Soviets. Sd.Kfz 250 halftracks with pintle-mounted MG34 machine guns worked in cooperation with the StuG IIIs, laying down suppressing fire to keep antitank infantry at bay.

The Germans also utilized heavy artillery concentrations, with rolling barrages moving just ahead of their troops and smoke screens deployed to block Soviet lines of sight. A Wehrmacht participant later recalled the action: "[N]ow we looked calmly at the towers on the horizon and knew for sure that it would not be long before we would climb those towers of Kiev. […] Friendly shells of all calibers were roaring over us. […] Then our smoke shells were fired. In front of the Bolshevik positions an enormous smoke screen expanded, as if suddenly a large theater curtain was dropped in front of the enemy. This was the signal for the […] infantrymen to attack." (Haupt, 1998, 80-81).

The Soviet artillery answered, sometimes hitting the Germans, but often suffering from lack of well-trained forward observers and simply pounding areas of terrain that the Germans avoided.

The Wehrmacht's gunners provided counter-battery fire also, gradually silencing the fire of the Soviet guns. All the while, commissars and other political officers roamed through the Soviet lines, shooting men who tried to fall back from their positions. As the situation deteriorated, the Soviets retreated anyway, or surrendered, sometimes killing their unit's commissar as a prelude in order to prevent being gunned down by him.

Several days of heavy fighting carried the Germans forward through the deep defensive lines encircling Kiev. On September 19, with multiple divisions piercing the city's defenses, Soviet resistance finally began to suffer irreversible collapse. Major General Wilhelm Stemmermann's 296th Infantry Division burst through the northern defenses close to the Dnieper's banks, penetrating almost 16 miles during the morning of the 19th. At the same time, the 95th Infantry Division and 99th Rifle Division pushed into the southern suburbs of Kiev, then fought their way into the streets. Elements of these two divisions reached the city center at around 11:00 a.m. There, they triumphantly raised the Kriegsflagge of the Third Reich – a variant on the standard Swastika flag with four black and white arms forming a crucifix-like quartering of the field behind the main emblem, and the Iron Cross of the German military in the canton. The Germans officially took Kiev on the 19th of September, though patchy combat continued for days as Soviet units made last stands here and there in the streets.

The German commanders and men felt the elation natural to soldiers overcoming a difficult obstacle, but Kiev had one more surprise in store for them. The Soviets left a number of large explosive devices hidden in the metropolis, which they detonated remotely following their departure. The Soviet engineers placed this ordnance in the buildings they deemed most likely to be occupied by the Germans, including an arsenal building near the famous Monastery of the

Caves. The Soviets also booby trapped the Grand Hotel and other locations likely to house German officers.

The Germans, delighted at finding the buildings intact, moved into precisely those structures the Soviets had prepared with lethal masses of explosives. Soon the explosions began, taking a heavy toll on the unprepared invaders. A huge cache of explosives demolished the Grand Hotel, blowing dozens of German officers, including Colonel Hans Heinrich Ferdinand Freiherr von Seydlitz und Gohlau of the Wehrmacht General Staff, to fragments.

These "parting gifts," according to some historians, helped trigger the Einsatzgruppen massacre at Babi Yar. General Gotthard Heinrici briefly noted the booby traps in a letter written to his wife on September 29th, with a pertinent afterthought: "The situation in Kiev is […] quite unpleasant, because the Russians have hidden a great amount of mines and incendiary devices which cause lots of detonations. The kind of warfare we witness here has nothing to do with a decent battle." (Hurter, 2014, 89).

The remote control detonations took place on September 24th, setting fire to large tracts of the city. All told, the Soviet demolition experts and saboteurs did their work well; walls of flame roared through conquered Kiev so rapidly that they trapped and killed as many as 200 German soldiers, burning them to death alongside the luckless inhabitants. Only after five days did the conflagrations burn out or succumb to fire extinguishing efforts.

In addition to the explosives which actually detonated, the Germans and Ukrainians assisting them located 670 more incendiary charges, many equipped with timers. Red Army saboteurs also remained in the city, carrying out arson attacks with Molotov cocktails. Other charges which the Germans failed to locate continued exploding sporadically through the middle of October, leveling more housing and leaving at least 15,000 Ukrainians without shelter at the onset of winter.

The destruction of much of their city, and the Soviets' attempt to firebomb their much-prized opera house, rekindled the rage of the Ukrainians, smoldering in any case after the 3.9 million deaths of the communists' genocidal Holomodor in the early 1930s and the political repression and death squads following it. General Heinrici noted the effects of Soviet rule on the Ukrainians: "[T]he first thing the village folk ask is: When do we get our land back that has been taken away from us? […] Everybody tries to display a poor lifestyle in order not to be persecuted or shot as a property owner. […] Even worse, however, is the people's fear of the party and its representatives. No one dares to do anything on their own responsibility, but waits for an order so as not to be punished." (Hurter, 2014, 81).

The Germans arrogantly failed to notice or exploit this anti-Soviet feeling, which could have netted them tens of thousands of recruits, or, at minimum, the willing assistance of an anti-communist population. Instead, the Germans swept the city for hunting rifles and other civilian arms which might be used to resist them, and instituted a savage martial rule. Ultimately, many of the Ukrainians managed to conceal their civilian rifles, supplemented by weapons scavenged secretly from the battlefield, to begin a fierce partisan movement. The vigorous partisan warfare generated by the Germans' harrowing treatment of the local inhabitants would prove a thorn in the Wehrmacht's side and greatly increase the difficulties of resupply.

After accelerating the process of destroying the Southwest Front, expending precious months in the process, Guderian turned his Panzer Group II northeast for Hitler's belated drive on Moscow. In the meantime, Army Group South pushed onward to the limits of its endurance, taking the industrial region between Kiev and Kharkov and seizing the Crimea, but failing to take Kharkov itself or the Donbas industrial region in 1941.

A picture of some of Kiev's ruins

Chapter 7: The Aftermath of the Battle

While the final drama was playing out in Kiev, the Germans continued their relentless compression of the encirclement along the perimeter. The two large pockets soon became three smaller ones, along with a handful of fragmentary holdouts, all firmly gripped in the claws of Panzer Groups I and II and their supporting infantry armies.

Timoshenko had authorized a full withdrawal to Psel on September 16th, but the maneuver was no longer feasible at that point for most of the men inside the pocket. Kirponos refused to believe the authorization carried any weight. Still anticipating a firing squad if he withdrew, he asked for explicit permission from Moscow for the retreat. Late on September 17th, Stalin transmitted grudging approval for the abandonment of Kiev, but specified no other acceptable retreat, leaving Kirponos once again in an impossible bind.

The Germans now began crushing the remaining pockets, where the Soviets, densely packed into dwindling islands of terrain, made ideal targets for Stuka formations and panzer attacks. A 3rd Panzer Division medic described the shambles in one such pocket near Kiev on September 19th: "Chaos reigns. Hundreds of trucks and cars, interspersed with tanks, are scattered over the land. Often the occupants were overcome by fire when they tried to get out and they hang from the doors, burned into black mummies. Thousands of corpses lay around the vehicles (Haupt, 1998, 82).

With no hope left, Mikhail Kirponos attempted to escape the trap on September 20th, 1941. Accompanied by 2,000 men from the Soviet 5th Army and the Southwestern Front headquarters unit, Kirponos reached Drukovshina, 9 miles south of Lochvitsa, before Wehrmacht units caught him, tantalizingly close to safety. Elements of the German 3rd Panzer Division spotted the Soviet convoy and rolled forward to the attack. The deafening crack of tank guns and the thunder of exploding shells rang out as the panzers went into action. Moments later, the vicious clatter of machine guns and the snap of rifles joined the din. The heavy, skillfully directed German fire quickly began to break up the Soviet column.

Soviet anti-tank gunners set up their weapons to fire on the advancing panzers, but high explosive shells smashed the guns and tore the crews to bloody ribbons. The Germans also quickly knocked out the thin-skinned BA-10 and BA-20 armored cars accompanying the convoy. Seeking a defensible position, the Soviets retreated into Shumeikovo Woods, a clump of forest near a collective farm.

The Russians fought desperately for their lives, using the trees and a ravine as cover. The equally determined Wehrmacht soldiers closed in, and a furious gun-battle lasting five hours followed. The Soviet officers fought alongside their troops, and the Germans killed Kirponos in action when they opened fire with mortars: "German mortar shells exploded all around, and, although Kirponos was soon wounded, he continued to direct his forces […] the Soviet troops not only repelled the enemy attacks but also launched occasional counterattacks of their own. Suddenly General Kirponos […] quietly groaned and slumped over on his side, as yet another shell fragment struck the commander's body. Kirponos died within two minutes." (Maslov, 1998, 27).

The Soviet soldiers, still desperately holding off the Germans, buried the Colonel-General in a hastily excavated grave near a stream. As the Germans finally broke through the defending lines on the eastern side of the woodland, most of the surviving Soviets shot themselves rather than be captured. Nevertheless, the Wehrmacht took several hundred prisoners, including the Soviet 5th Army commander, Lieutenant General M.I. Potapov, who had been knocked unconscious by the shock of a mortar shell exploding nearby.

In a strange footnote to Kirponos' death, a commissar escaped from the encirclement carrying the commander's comb and pocket mirror. He brought these objects to Khrushchev, then at Poltava, east of the encirclement. After receiving these personal effects of the dead general, Khrushchev talked with the commissar further: "He said there was still a chance to penetrate to those areas. I asked him, since there was such a possibility, to go back and remove from Kirponos's service jacket his Gold Star signifying Hero of the Soviet Union. He had always worn it. And the man did go! There were marshes in the area that were hard to cross with mechanized equipment, but this man overcame those obstacles and returned, bringing the Gold Star with him." (Khrushchev, 2005, 344).

One of the last high-ranking officers to escape the encirclement alive, Lieutenant General Fyodor Kostenko, reported that the people along the way fed and sheltered him and the small band of men accompanying him. Kirill Moskalenko, by contrast, who escaped a few days earlier, attempted to hide in a cowshed, from which a peasant woman wielding a pitchfork had evicted him. Those who eluded the trap barely succeeded in doing so, whether they were common soldiers or generals; many others found themselves forced to surrender, or died either deep within the crushed salient or close to escape in the manner of Kirponos.

In the short term, the Battle of Kiev reaped spectacular results for the Germans, destroying a large portion of the remaining Red Army that had existed at the start of Operation Barbarossa. While deaths are unknown – but assuredly a vast total – the Red Army suffered 85,000 wounded, and the Germans claimed no less than 665,000 Soviet soldiers captured. In response to the colossal numbers of prisoners taken during the operation, Hitler engaged in bombastic flights of fancy: "I declare today – and I declare it without reservation – the enemy in the East has been struck down and will never rise again." (Axell, 1997, 182).

Anyone who knows a trivial amount about World War II knows how Germany's invasion of the Soviet Union ends, but as just about every history written about this battle and Operation Barbarossa as a whole readily indicates, far from representing an inevitable loss, the German invasion bore many of the hallmarks of a highly successful campaign carried out with forethought, a superb degree of professionalism, and the conception and execution of a logistically supported *Schwerpunkt* on a titanic scale. The comparison between Napoleon's and Hitler's campaigns too often obscures the profound differences between the two invasions of Russia, especially when German planners carefully researched Napoleon's campaign in order to avoid its mistakes well before the operation was underway.

The main advance of the Germans, centered on driving towards Moscow, did not suffer defeat due to either the size of Russia or the Soviet opposition. The Wehrmacht smashed the Soviets in nearly every encounter during the opening months, while their few setbacks had essentially no strategic importance. The German work battalions performed magnificently, driving railways forward quickly enough to keep Army Group Center fully supplied even as it moved rapidly from the Third Reich's previous border. Using the railways and the immense, well-organized masses of trucks extending their logistic reach, the Wehrmacht pushed railways as far as Smolensk, establishing a massive railhead there. The Germans' method of defeating the spaces of the Soviet Union consisted of extremely rapid railroad construction. This technique represented a viable way to overcome the challenges that defeated the earlier invader, Napoleon, who lacked such technology.

The use of strategic military railway-building brought the Germans within striking distance of Moscow by early August, after shattering most of the Red Army. And unlike Napoleon's campaign, which seized the city to virtually no effect in 1812, the Nazi capture of Moscow would have had a profound impact on the course of the Eastern Front. In the early 19th century, a capital city merely represented a large concentration of people. In the 20th century, however, Moscow held a considerable portion of the Soviet Union's manufacturing capability – as much as 25% – and represented a key rail hub for the entirety of European Russia. Had the Germans seized it, they would have attained a stranglehold on the supply lines for Leningrad and other peripheral areas and forces, compelling their surrender or weakening them enough for rapid destruction.

If anything, Adolf Hitler himself represented the single factor preventing a crushing victory of the Wehrmacht over the Soviet Union in summer 1941. Hitler created strategic plans of sweeping boldness, then, once in motion, flinched away from the decisive encounter, halting or diverting his forces. The Fuhrer did the same twice in France alone, halting the panzer drive to the coast, and then, more disastrously, stopping his men short of crushing the British Expeditionary Force at Dunkirk. In France, the Germans remained overwhelming enough that the mistakes did not punish Hitler's glaring errors; France fell nevertheless and the Fuhrer learned nothing.

During Operation Barbarossa, Hitler launched his mechanized divisions at Moscow, then, against the advice of most of his generals, shrank away from the crucial battle which would almost certainly have given him victory in the east. Instead, he diffused the steely tidal bore of the Wehrmacht advance into many feeble eddies, spending its force on secondary objectives and waiting until the autumn mud and the onset of winter before resuming the drive on Moscow. When the Fuhrer shrank from dealing a potential deathblow to the USSR by taking Moscow in summer rather than dispersing the Ostheer's energy in attacks on Leningrad and Kiev, he cast away the war-winning opportunity Operation Barbarossa delivered to him within two months of crossing the Soviet Union's border. Simultaneously, he ensured the eventual defeat of the Third Reich in a war of attrition that hampered its unique military strengths while exploiting its material weaknesses.

Thus, while the Battle of Kiev represented a large-scale operational victory for the Germans, in hindsight it proved to be a Pyrrhic victory given the grand picture of Barbarossa itself. By cold-blooded strategic analysis, Moscow had a far higher value than the lives or freedom of a million Soviet soldiers in Ukraine. Moscow represented the main rail hub for the entire Soviet railway system, without which the Soviet armies would be logistically crippled for a dangerously long time. Additionally, the Moscow area included key industries such as major tank and ammunition factories. By delaying "Operation Typhoon", the attack towards Moscow, until after the autumn raputitsa and the bitter winter weather following it, the First Battle of Kiev unwittingly helped the Soviets make a desperate last stand across the Eastern Front in 1942.

A notable operational success for the Germans and a frequently overlooked battle despite its enormous scale, the First Battle of Kiev occurred as it did because of major errors by the two enemy dictators. Stalin had ordered his men to stand firm in an untenable position, leading to vast losses, while Hitler crippled an attack on Moscow that may very well have won the Eastern Front outright. Stalin recovered from his gaffe in time, while Hitler's botching of Barbarossa, against the advice of his generals, proved fatal. Once again, the battle of Kiev demonstrated the truth of Napoleon Bonaparte's maxim: "The greatest general is he who makes the least mistakes."

Online Resources

Other books about World War II by Charles River Editors

Other books about the Battle of Kiev on Amazon

Bibliography

Axell, Albert. Stalin's War: Through the Eyes of the Commanders. London, 1997.

Berkhoff, Karel C. Harvest of Despair: Life and Death in Ukraine under Nazi Rule. Cambridge, 2004.

Bidermann, Gottlob Herbert, and Derek S. Zumbro (translator). In Deadly Combat: A German Soldier's Memoir of the Eastern Front. Lawrence, 2000.

Forczyk, Robert. Tank Warfare on the Eastern Front 1941-1942: Schwerpunkt. Barnsley, 2013.

Guderian, Heinz and Constantine Fitzgibbon (translator). Panzer Leader. Cambridge, 1996.

Haupt, Werner, and Joseph G. Welsh (translator). Army Group South: The Wehrmacht in Russia, 1941-1945. Atglen, 1998.

Hurter, Johannes, and Christine Brocks (translator). A German General on the Eastern Front: The Letters and Diaries of Gotthard Heinrici, 1941-1942. Barnsley, 2014.

Kirchubel, Robert. Operation Barbarossa 1941 (1): Army Group South. Oxford, 2003.

Khrushchev, Sergei (editor). Memoirs of Nikita Khrushchev, Volume 1: Commissar, 1918-1945. University Park, 2005.

Lucas, James. Das Reich: Military Role of the 2nd SS Division. London, 1991.

Maslov, Aleksander A. and David M. Glantz (translator). Fallen Soviet Generals: Soviet General Officers Killed in Battle, 1941-1945. Portland, 1998.

Stahel, David. Kiev 1941: Hitler's Battle for Supremacy in the East. New York, 2012.

Stahl, Erich. Eyewitness to Hell: With the Waffen-SS on the Eastern Front in World War 2. Seattle, 2010.

Stolfi, R.H.S. Hitler's Panzers East: World War II Reinterpreted. Norman, 1992.

Free Books by Charles River Editors

We have brand new titles available for free most days of the week. To see which of our titles are currently free, click on this link.

Discounted Books by Charles River Editors

We have titles at a discount price of just 99 cents everyday. To see which of our titles are currently 99 cents, click on this link.

Printed in Great Britain
by Amazon